URANUS

PLANETS IN OUR SOLAR SYSTEM

CHILDREN'S ASTRONOMY EDITION

SPEEDY
PUBLISHING

Speedy Publishing LLC
40 E. Main St. #1156
Newark, DE 19711
www.speedypublishing.com

Uranus is the seventh planet from the Sun.

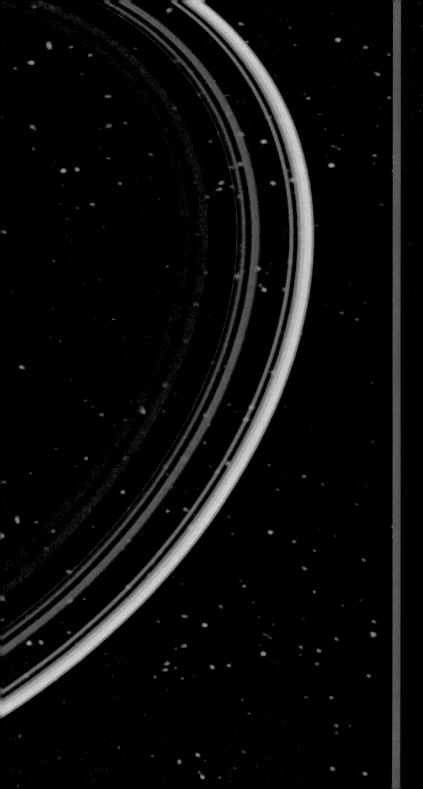

Uranus has the third-largest planetary radius and fourth-largest planetary mass in the Solar System.

Uranus's mass is roughly 14.5 times that of Earth.

It is mostly
made of
hydrogen and
helium, but
methane gas
gives it its vivid
blue color.

It has the coldest
planetary atmosphere
in the Solar System.

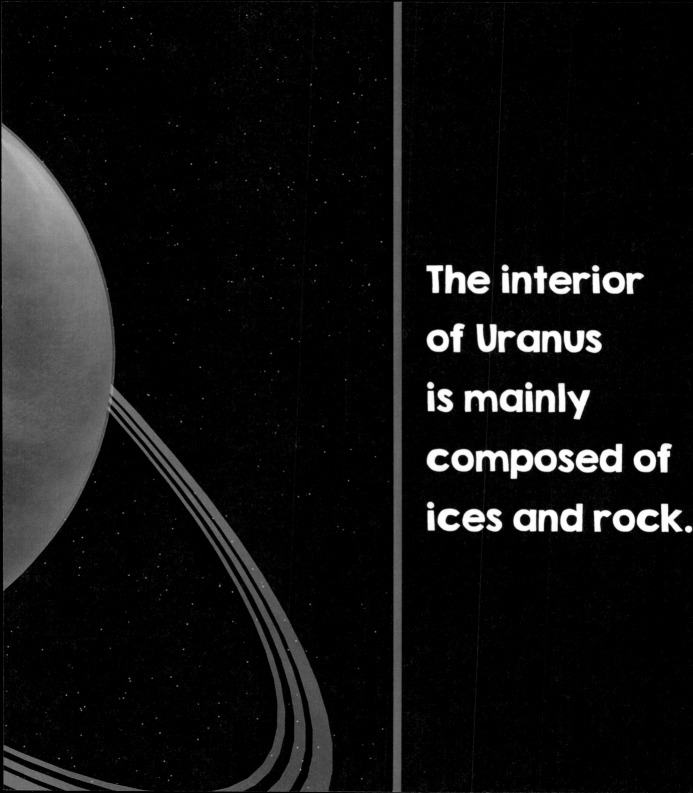

The interior
of Uranus
is mainly
composed of
ices and rock.

Uranus was the first planet discovered by telescope.

Uranus is named after the ancient Greek deity of the sky Uranus.

Uranus was first seen
by William Herschel
in 1781 during a
survey of the sky
using a telescope.

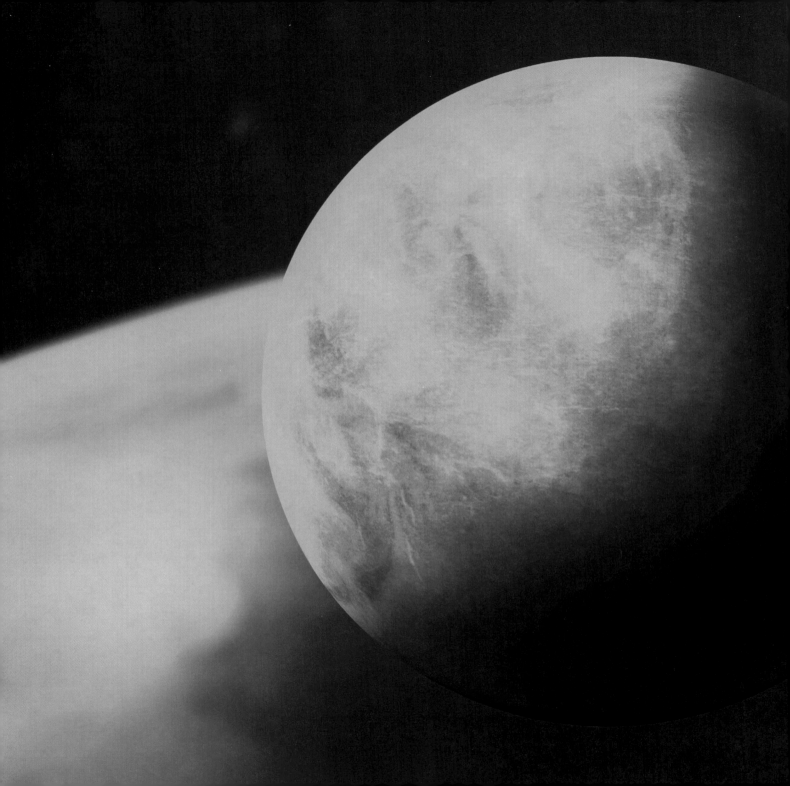

Uranus orbits
the Sun once
every 84
Earth years.

Uranus' most unique features is that it rotates on its side.

Uranus takes
17.9 hours to
turn once on
its own axis.

Uranus is often referred to as an "ice giant" planet.

Uranus also has rings, thirteen distinct rings are presently known. The rings are composed of extremely dark particles.

If you weigh 32 kg
on Earth, you would
weigh 28 kg on Uranus.

Uranus is 2,869 million kilometres away from the Sun.

Uranus' moons are
named after characters
created by William
Shakespeare and
Alaxander Pope.

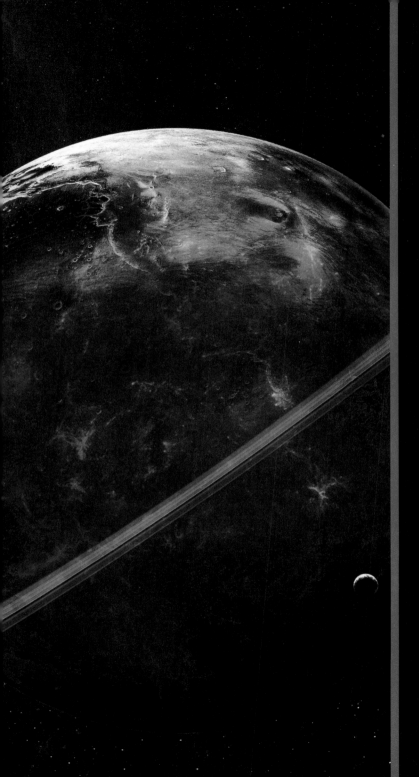

Uranus has 27 known natural satellites. The five main satellites are Miranda, Ariel, Umbriel, Titania, and Oberon.

Only one spacecraft has flown by Uranus. NASA's Voyager 2 zipped past Uranus in January, 1986.

Made in United States
North Haven, CT
14 March 2023

34060510R00024